The Life of
Paul Revere/

La vida de
Paul Revere

By Maria Nelson   **Traducción al español: Eduardo Alamán**

Gareth Stevens
Publishing

Please visit our website, www.garethstevens.com. For a free color catalog of all our high-quality books, call toll free 1-800-542-2595 or fax 1-877-542-2596.

Library of Congress Cataloging-in-Publication Data

Nelson, Maria.
[Life of Paul Revere. Spanish & English]
The life of Paul Revere = La vida de Paul Revere / Maria Nelson.
    p. cm. — (Famous lives = Vidas extraordinarias)
Includes index.
ISBN 978-1-4339-6657-6 (library binding)
1. Revere, Paul, 1735-1818—Juvenile literature. 2. Massachusetts—History—Revolution, 1775-1783—Juvenile literature. 3. Statesmen—Massachusetts—Biography—Juvenile literature. 4. Massachusetts—Biography—Juvenile literature. I. Title. II. Title: Vida de Paul Revere.
F69.R43N4518 2012
974.4'03092—dc23
[B]

                                        2011039809

First Edition

Published in 2012 by
Gareth Stevens Publishing
111 East 14th Street, Suite 349
New York, NY 10003

Copyright © 2012 Gareth Stevens Publishing

Designer: Daniel Hosek
Editor: Kristen Rajczak
Spanish translation: Eduardo Alamán

Photo credits: Cover, pp. 1, 13 MPI/Getty Images; p. 5 Kean Collection/Getty Images; p. 7 Mansell/Time & Life Pictures/Getty Images; pp. 9, 11 Three Lions/Hulton Archive/Getty Images; p. 15 Thinkstock.com; p. 17 SuperStock/Getty Images; p. 19 Masterfile.com; p. 21 iStockphoto.com.

Printed in the United States of America

CPSIA compliance information: Batch #CW12GS: For further information contact Gareth Stevens, New York, New York at 1-800-542-2595.

Contents

Contenido

Boldface words appear in the glossary/
Las palabras en **negrita** aparecen en el glosario

American Hero

Paul Revere was an American **patriot**. Like many patriots of his time, he wanted America to be free from British rule. He bravely **warned** a town that the British army was coming.

- -

Un héroe estadounidense

Paul Revere fue un **patriota** estadounidense. Como muchos otros patriotas de su época, Revere quería que los Estados Unidos se liberaran del control de la Gran Bretaña. Mostrando gran valor, Revere le **avisó** a un poblado que la armada británica se acercaba.

5

Life in the Colonies

Paul was born January 1, 1735. He lived in Boston, Massachusetts. During this time, Massachusetts was a British **colony**.

La vida en las colonias

Paul nació el primero de enero de 1735. Paul vivía en Boston, Massachusetts. En aquellos días, Massachusetts era una **colonia** británica.

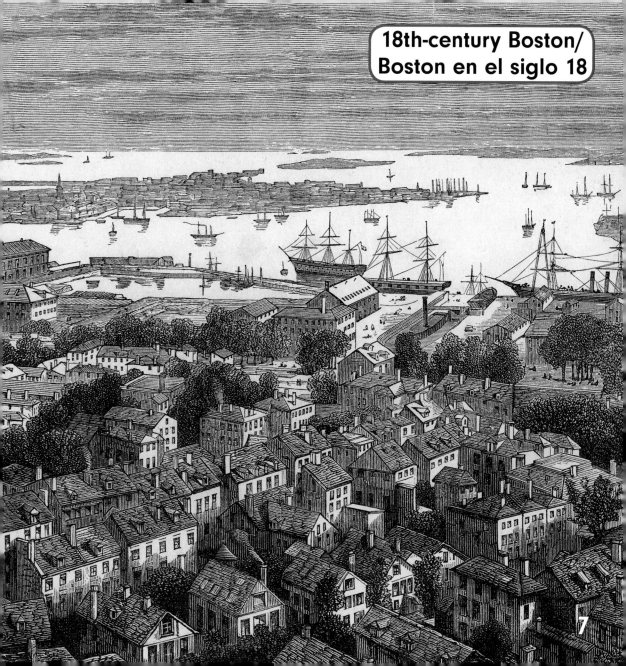

18th-century Boston/
Boston en el siglo 18

7

Paul's father was a **smith** who worked with gold and silver. He taught Paul to make forks and spoons, tea sets, and other objects. Paul took over the business after his father died.

El padre de Paul era un **orfebre** que trabajaba con oro y plata. Paul aprendió de su padre a hacer tenedores, cucharas, juegos de té y otros objetos. A la muerte de su padre, Paul se encargó del negocio.

9

In 1756, Paul fought for England in a war against France. The next year, he married Sarah Orne. She later died. Paul married Rachel Walker in 1773. He had many children.

In 1756, Paul peleó por Inglaterra en la guerra contra Francia. Al año siguiente se casó con Sarah Orne. Sarah Orne murió a los pocos años. En 1773. Paul se casó con Rachel Walker. La pareja tuvo muchos hijos.

A Patriot in Action

In 1773, a group of angry colonists threw British tea into Boston Harbor. This was called the Boston Tea Party. Paul was there! He and other patriots were unhappy with British laws.

Un patriota en acción

En 1773, un grupo de colonos, molestos con el gobierno británico, tiraron el té británico en el puerto de Boston. Esto se conoce como el Motín del Té de Boston. ¡Paul paticipó en el motín! Como muchos otros patriotas, Paul estaba molesto con las leyes británicas.

13

By 1775, many colonists wanted **revolution**! Paul and others planned to warn them if the British army was coming. Paul would carry a message. If he failed, one light in the **steeple** of Christ Church meant the army was coming by land. Two meant by sea.

Para el año 1775, muchos colonos querían la **independencia**. Paul y otros planearon una manera de avisar a los colonos cuando se acercaba la armada británica. Paul llevaría un mensaje. Si Paul fracasaba, dejaría una luz en el **chapitel** de la Iglesia de Jesucristo. Una luz quería decir que venían por tierra. Dos, quería decir que venían por mar.

The Midnight Ride

On the night of April 18, 1775, Paul learned the British army was coming to find two leaders of the revolution. He wanted to warn them! Paul crossed the Charles River by boat. He then rode a horse to Lexington, Massachusetts.

La cabalgata de la medianoche

En la noche del 18 de abril de 1775, Paul se enteró de que la armada británica trataría de encontrar a los líderes de la independencia. ¡Paul quería avisarles! Paul cruzó el río Charles en barco. Luego cabalgó hasta Lexington, Massachusetts.

17

Because of Paul's warning, the leaders escaped and the colonists were ready to fight! The Battle of Lexington and Concord was the first of the American Revolution.

¡Gracias a la cabalgata de Paul, los líderes lograron escapar y los colonos estuvieron listos para pelear! La batalla de Lexington y Concord fue la primera batalla de la Independencia de Estados Unidos.

19

The Poem

Paul died in 1818. In 1860, a writer named Henry Wadsworth Longfellow wrote a **poem** about him. It was called "Paul Revere's Ride." Today, many people still read about Paul's famous ride!

- -

El poema

Paul murió en 1818. En 1860, el escritor Henry Wadsworth Longfellow escribió un **poema** en su honor. El poema se llama "La cabalgata de Paul Revere". ¡Hoy, muchas personas leen sobre la famosa cabalgata!

Timeline/Cronología

1735 — Paul Revere is born on January 1./Primero de enero, nace Paul Revere.

1756 — Paul fights in England's war with France./ Paul pelea en la guerra de Inglaterra con Francia.

1773 — The Boston Tea Party takes place./ Se lleva a cabo el Motín del Té de Boston.

1775 — Paul warns colonial leaders that the British army is coming./Paul avisa a los líderes de la colonia que la armada británica se acerca.

1818 — Paul dies./ Muere Paul Revere.

Glossary/Glosario

colony: a piece of land under the control of another country. Someone who lives in a colony is a colonist.

patriot: a person who loves their country

poem: a piece of writing in verse that sometimes tells a story

revolution: the overthrow of a government

smith: a person who works with metals

steeple: a tall, pointed part on top of a building

warn: to let others know danger is coming

- -

avisar: decirle a otros que algo va a suceder.

chapitel (el): La parte alta y puntiaguda de un edificio.

colonia (la): un territorio controlado por otro país. Una persona que vive en una colonia es un colono.

independencia (la): separarse de un gobierno.

orfebre (el/la): persona que trabaja en plata y otros metales.

patriota (el/la): una persona que ama a su país.

poema (el): una forma de escribir con rima.

For More Information/Más información

Books/Libros

Carson, Mary Kay. *Did It All Start with a Snowball Fight And Other Questions About the American Revolution*. New York, NY: Sterling Publishing Company, 2012.

Karapetkova, Holly. *Riding with Paul Revere*. Vero Beach, FL: Rourke Publishing, 2010.

Web Sites/Páginas en Internet

The Paul Revere House

www.paulreverehouse.org
Learn more about Paul Revere and where he lived.

Paul Revere's Ride

poetry.eserver.org/paul-revere.html
Read Longfellow's poem about Paul Revere's famous ride.

Index/Índice

- -